CAPRICORN

CAPRICORN

December 22–January 19

NAME

SUN SIGN

MOON SIGN

RISING SIGN

Crystal Astrology for Modern Life

SANDY SITRON

CONTENTS

CAPRICORN
THROUGHOUT
THE YEAR

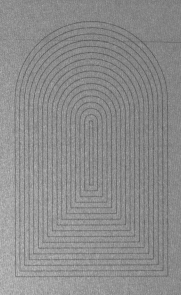

LUNAR
ENERGY AND
MERCURY IN MOTION

CRYSTALS, ASTROLOGY AND YOU

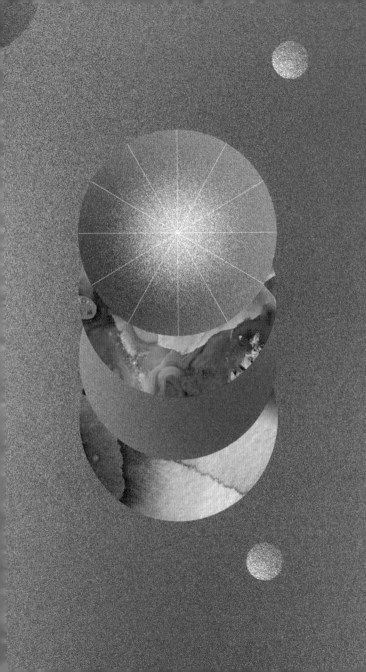

THE STONES,
THE SIGNS AND YOU

The stars above you and the stones beneath your feet are part of the fabric of your world. Astrology offers a cosmic perspective. Crystals radiate with the healing energy of the Earth. Together, they serve as guides in your life, engaged in a vibrational conversation that can help you reflect on, and tune into, who you are. Birthstones and other crystals can be used to highlight and harness the energy of your astrological birth chart.

As above, so below – harness the power of crystals and the cosmos to create a deeper connection with yourself for a confident, empowered, high-vibe life.

Astrology is the ancient study of the changing positions and alternating energy of the celestial bodies and how this relates to our lives on Earth. The unique cosmic environment that you synced up with at the moment of your first breath provides awareness of – and offers a way to interpret – your personality traits, core strengths, growth areas, emotional style and so much more. When you better understand your vibrational self, it's easier to make informed choices about the big and small things in your life. Your conscious perspective is uplifted. Your mind is opened and activated.

Crystals, or 'stones', vibrate with the breath of the Earth. They act on an energetic level, sending vibrations out into the world. They are natural amplifiers of positive energy and bring discordant energies into balance. Each crystal has its own energy blueprint, which is why different types of stones may influence the human energy field in different ways. Pairing the insight that you gain from astrology with the healing power of crystals can help you navigate certain life areas and facilitate personal transformation and spiritual growth throughout the astrological year.

Crystals and the constellations call to us. In this book you'll receive a bespoke selection of crystals to help you amplify or balance the unique energies of your sign. You'll gain insight into your life, activate your highest potential and learn to live harmoniously with the energy that surrounds you.

When gazing at the night sky, when you hold a crystal in your hand, feel inspired to slow down, be present in the moment and get ready to embark on a meaningful journey of self-discovery.

YOUR UNIQUE RECOMMENDATIONS

We all accept that different things work for different people. Advice that's a perfect fit for one person might fall flat for someone else. Regardless of where Capricorn sits in your personal astrology, this book will help you understand your Capricorn nature and give you specific crystal recommendations for your sign and each astrological season. You can use these bespoke Capricorn crystals to build confidence, spark creativity, feel more present, harmonize relationships, attract love, embrace your emotions, cultivate friendships, create abundance, optimize your health and wellness, amplify your natural gifts and find balance.

YOUR ASTRO-CRYSTAL JOURNEY

Once you understand how the two energetic studies of crystals and astrology relate to your life, you'll be ready to take a deep dive into your Capricorn energy and learn to use crystals to leverage the strengths of your Capricorn gifts, whether Capricorn is your Sun, Moon or Rising sign, or elsewhere in your unique astrology. You'll also discover your unique Capricorn crystal recommendations for love, friendship, money, work and health to help you connect to your true potential and reach your dreams and goals.

As each astrological season holds a different kind of energy, this book will take you through the year and show you how crystals can help you channel your unique Capricorn energy under each sign. In this way, you will learn to navigate through the seasons with ease and to harmonize with the cycles of nature. You will discover how crystals can help you embrace the ebb and flow of the 29-day Moon cycle, enable you to sail through Mercury Retrograde and even plan your week.

This book is part of a series that unites each of the twelve zodiac signs with recommended crystals. When you are ready to go deeper on your astro-crystal journey, you may choose to purchase the companion books in the series that correspond to the other prominent signs in your birth chart.

THE
STONES

Dazzling gemstones are typically formed deep under the Earth's surface, stimulated by the combination of mineral-rich water, heat and pressure. Subterranean 'gardens' nurture the formation of billions of atoms into highly ordered, three-dimensional repeating patterns to create unique crystals, each one holding a vibrational record of earthly, physical reality.

Across the world and over millennia, people have been fascinated by crystals. Lucent jewels have captured the imagination for over 30,000 years. In the Democratic Republic of the Congo, small tools decorated with Quartz have been found that date back to 33,000 BCE. The Ancient Sumerians of Mesopotamia (present-day Iraq) used crystals for rituals and magic in the fourth century BCE. Humankind has used crystals for decoration, status, currency, religion, healing, magic-making and, in more recent times, modern technology. Early radios used crystals as electrical and tuning components. Today's computers, LCD screens and some batteries rely on crystal technology.

Good Vibrations   People across different cultures and generations have turned to crystals as guides or helpers because it seems that, whatever facet of earthly experience you are struggling with, there is a crystal frequency that can help you move forwards on your path. Crystals may help bring calm and heal stress, empower you when you need support or confidence, or provide focus and clarity when you're struggling with an important decision. Crystals are thought to absorb the energy that you are trying to release and release the energy you are trying to absorb.

For example, if you are feeling dull and listless, Carnelian may share with you a vibration of high energy and drive. If you are overheated or stressed, Rose Quartz may help you soften and relax. Choosing the right crystal that resonates with, or reacts to, your energy can shift your mood or your mindset.

CHOOSING YOUR CRYSTALS

In Part Two of this book, you will be guided to a selection of crystals that are energetically aligned with your unique astrology. If you are adding these stones to your collection, it's important to choose responsibly.

Sustainability and Ethics   How did the crystal that you have in your hand make its way to you? The answer to this question is incredibly important to the well-being of humanity and the Earth.

The crystal industry is shrouded in mystery and plagued by bad practices. When you purchase a crystal, make sure to find gems that have a traceable, and short, journey from the mine to your hand. It's important to know if the mine that the crystal came from uses ethical, safe and sustainable practices. Discover if the lapidary, where the crystal was cut and polished, is a safe place that pays a living wage to the people who work there. The easiest way to do this is to mindfully source your crystals from sellers who have done the legwork. You vote with your financial choices. Make sure that you are contributing to better health and safety for all.

More information about sustainable and ethical practices and purveyors can be found on my website www.sandysitron.com/crystals.

Size, Finish and Price   When harnessing the power of a crystal for personal use, the size of the stone doesn't matter. If you are holding a crystal or carrying it close to your body, its vibration is in your energy field and will have an effect whatever its size.

A raw stone is a stone that is untreated. These are just as effective to use in healing practices as a crystal that has been tumbled or polished. So when you are choosing a crystal, choose one that appeals to you, no matter the size or finish.

The stones selected in this book can be sourced at an affordable price. Although some of the stones mentioned may sound ultra-luxurious and expensive, these crystals are available at a range of values.

YOUR CRYSTAL TOOLKIT

In the next section, you'll find crystal
recommendations for your specific sign. First,
here are a few indispensable crystals to round out your
toolkit. These selections are a wonderful support for
anyone at any time.

GROUNDING
AND PROTECTION

CLEANSING
YOUR ENERGY

Smoky Quartz Getting grounded is the basis of spiritual work. So many factors in everyday life pull us out of ourselves. Spending too much time on your phone, not enough time in nature or eating too much sugar are common culprits, but the list goes on. If you want to nail your next meeting at work, remember where your keys are, or get on top of that to-do list, you need to get grounded. Feeling grounded also allows you to be present in your relationships and tuned in to your physical needs. This is where Smoky Quartz can help. This crystal keeps you centred, and emotionally clear. It may help you take a more practical view of a situation. On a more mystical level, Smoky Quartz has the effect of protecting you from energetic drains on your system. It is an excellent protection stone and just holding it can help you feel steady.

Selenite Just as you bathe your body regularly, it makes sense to regularly cleanse your energy system too. Energetic cleansing can help you balance your emotions and clear your mind. Cleanse your energy after work, socializing or spending time in a crowd. Or employ Selenite to help you get rid of emotional residue after a tough conversation. Energy cleansing is also recommended when you are going through any kind of transition – a break-up, a move or some other important milestone. Use Selenite with the intention of purifying your energy field and cleansing yourself of anything that is dragging you down. Imagine that it shines a ray of light through your entire body, clearing and cleansing.

Smoky Quartz Ritual	Selenite Ritual
Perform the grounding practice on page 26 while holding Smoky Quartz to anchor you.	Selenite can also be used to cleanse the energy of your other stones. Place a Selenite stone next to your crystals overnight.

SOOTHING
RELAXATION

Rose Quartz   We all know what it's
like to get stressed out and frazzled.
Sometimes the nervous system is
overloaded and it's hard to calm
down. When that happens, you need a
soothing crystal ally that can help you
relax. If you are having trouble sleeping,
are feeling on edge, or are working
through some challenging emotions,
it's time to soften with Rose Quartz.
This dreamy pink stone is known for its
inherent ability to calm and reassure.
It soothes you while strengthening your
capacity for empathy and compassion.
If you're feeling down, lonely or
heartbroken, let this crystalline stress-
reliever support you.

FINDING
YOUR DIRECTION

Clear Quartz   Clear quartz is a true
all-purpose stone. When you actively
set an intention with Clear Quartz,
the stone will magnify that intention.
When your world is changing around
you and you need to forge ahead in
a new direction, Clear Quartz will
get you there. Clear Quartz can
help you clarify, strategize and set
your aspirations for your life. Once
programmed with your wishes and
desires, this powerful amplifier will
hold the vibration of your intentions
and help you visualize and realize
your future.

Rose Quartz Ritual	Clear Quartz Ritual
Infuse a tumbled Rose Quartz stone in your next cup of tea or glass of water for a mindful moment with a soothing elixir.	Write an affirmation that inspires you. Say your affirmation aloud while holding Clear Quartz.

Amethyst Your intuition is your natural guidance system. It's that gut feeling you have when something feels wrong, or when something feels just right. Intuition shows up in different ways for everyone but it's like a muscle that can be strengthened. If you have questions about your life and you want to tune into the answers, Amethyst is at your service. In those moments, practice asking and listening and let this violet stone help open up your mind's eye. Amethyst is also a fantastic friend when you need help saying the right thing in your next important conversation, meeting or presentation. Or if you are looking for a sparkling boost to your creativity, open the channels of inspiration with Amethyst by your side.

	Amethyst Ritual	

The next time you have a question about your life or
path, lie down and place an Amethyst stone on your forehead or
near the crown of your head. Meditate and make space for
the answer to come through.

THE SIGNS

ASTROLOGY AND YOU

You are a unique being, made up of a solar system of characteristics that define your identity. Astrology illuminates your personality and your path. It describes how you think, learn, love, act and much more. Astrology can also be used to understand the energy of the moment.

Astrology has been contributed to by cultures throughout the world over thousands of years. The astrology used in this book is drawn from contemporary Western astrology. Like all things in the universe, the movements of the planets through the zodiac create a vibration. At the moment of your first breath, this energy is mirrored within you.

Your astrology is much more complex than just your star sign. The movements of the planets under the zodiac, in the exact place, at the exact moment you were born form your birth chart, a personalized map of the sky from your unique vantage point on Earth when you took your first breath. As well as showing you where the Sun lands in your chart, denoting your star sign, it also shows under which signs the Moon and other planets fall – this is the key to understanding your personal energetic code.

In order to discover your unique astrological make-up first you need to map your birth chart.

SUN, MOON AND RISING SIGN

When someone asks, 'What's your sign?' they are actually referring to your Sun sign, but it's worth learning your Moon and Rising signs too. These three symbols are a good place to begin your astrological journey as they represent the basic outline of who you are – like a simple sketch that captures your likeness in just a few brushstrokes. Together these three symbols make up your inner and outer self.

Casting Your Birth Chart Go to www.sandysitron.com/crystals and enter your birth data in the 'Create Your Birth Chart' tool. You'll then receive your birth chart, also called your natal chart, that shows the signs that the planets were in when you were born, and where they were located in the sky.

SUN SIGN

The Sun is a constant bright light, it symbolizes your ego, the part of you that you consciously identify with. It's how you tend to think of yourself.

The Sun is the gravitational centre of the solar system, it represents your core self and describes your fundamental character and values.

The Sun is the energy source that creates life on our planet, it signifies how you channel your energy.

RISING SIGN

· The Rising sign, also known as your Ascendant, is the constellation of the zodiac that was rising on the eastern horizon at the precise moment of your birth.

· The Rising sign shines new light into the world. It symbolizes how the rays of your personality beam out ahead as you walk down the street, meet new people, or interact on social media. It represents your vibe or your 'brand'. It epitomizes how other people see you.

· As you explore the following pages, you'll learn how to balance and enhance your unique energy using supportive crystals. This book will also help you find alignment and teach you how to leverage your inherent gifts.

MOON SIGN

The Moon is most visible at night, it symbolizes the part of you that is hard to see – your subconscious self.

The Moon changes shape through the lunar month. It represents your ever-changing emotions and how you respond subconsciously to your feelings.

The Moon is a satellite that circles the Earth, it describes how you turn inwards to protect, nurture and soothe yourself.

PLANETS

SUN
⊙

MOON
☽

MERCURY
☿

VENUS
♀

MARS
♂

JUPITER
♃

SATURN
♄

URANUS
♅

NEPTUNE
♆

PLUTO
♇

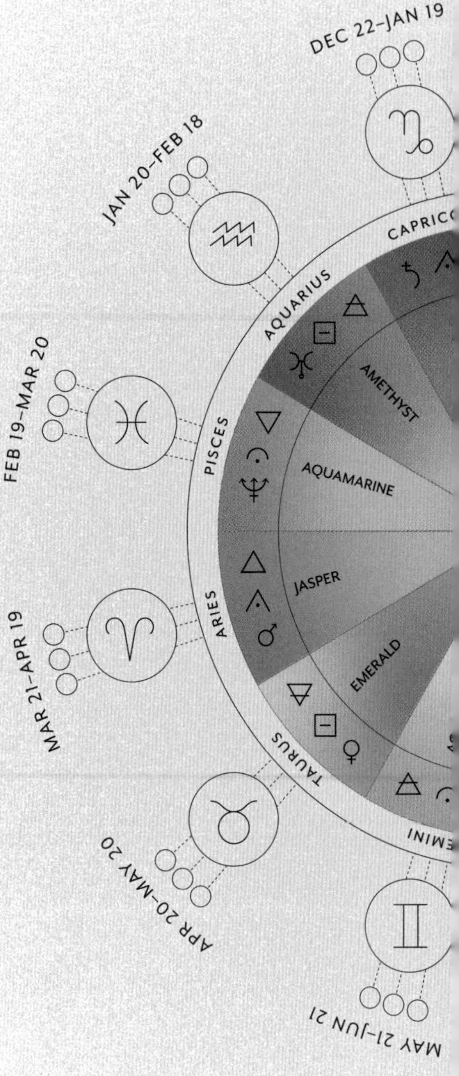

DEC 22–JAN 19
♑
CAPRICORN

JAN 20–FEB 18
♒
AQUARIUS

FEB 19–MAR 20
♓
PISCES

MAR 21–APR 19
♈
ARIES

APR 20–MAY 20
♉
TAURUS

MAY 21–JUN 21
♊
GEMINI

AMETHYST

AQUAMARINE

JASPER

EMERALD

DATES ARE APPROXIMATE AS THE DATES OF THE
SIGNS VARY BY ABOUT A DAY FROM YEAR TO YEAR.

NOV 22–DEC 21

OCT 24–NOV 21

SEP 23–OCT 23

AUG 23–SEP 22

JUL 23–AUG 22

JUN 22–JUL 22

SAGITTARIUS

SCORPIO

TOPAZ

OPAL

LIBRA

SAPPHIRE

VIRGO

CARNELIAN

LEO

CANCER

ELEMENTS

FIRE

△

EARTH

▽

AIR

△

WATER

▽

MODALITY

CARDINAL

∧

FIXED

□

MUTABLE

⌒

TOOLS FOR YOUR JOURNEY

As you go forwards on your astro-crystal journey, two key tools can help you gain insight and create positive change – intuition and intention. Intuition helps you know what you want and intention helps you make it happen.

LETTING YOUR
INTUITION GUIDE YOU

Everyone is intuitive, your intuition or 'inner knowing' is your built-in guidance system. Use the following prompts to strengthen your inner voice.

How to Connect
with Your Intuition

Slow down Take a few deep breaths and close your eyes. The more you can slow down in your life (even for just five minutes) the louder your intuitive voice grows.

Pose a question What do you want to know? Ask yourself. Say it aloud or ponder it silently. Or choose to write it down, sketch it or even dance it out. However you pose the question, make sure it is clear. If you aren't sure what to ask, try, 'what do I need to know that I don't yet know?'

Listen for the answer You might hear words or notice a sensation in your body. You might write down your question in a notebook then flip the page and write down the answer. You might have an emotional response or feel compelled to move in a certain way. Pay attention.

Practice The more you practice asking and listening, the more you get to understand your unique intuitive voice. Just as weightlifting tones your physical body, practicing these steps improves your intuitive muscle, so stick with it!

21

INTENTION
SETTING

In your meditations and rituals, you can program your crystals with the intentions or affirmations that will help you meet your goals.
An intention is a new thought that you would like to think. Our subconscious minds save energy by putting certain thoughts and habits on repeat. This survival skill has benefits, such as giving us more energy and space for other things, but it also has its downsides, such as getting us stuck in a negative pattern. One way to break in a new way of thinking is to intentionally repeat a new thought. Here is how to 'affirm' your new way of thinking into being!

Define what it is you would like to change. Where are you feeling stuck? What is the pattern that is bugging you? For example, 'I am stuck because I have these exciting ideas for new projects, but I never finish what I start.'

· Decide what you want
For instance, 'It would be great if I finished my projects.'

· Make it an 'I' statement
Such as, 'I finish my projects.'

· Make it affirmative
Make sure your affirmation is positively stated. Say what you want, not what you don't want. So 'I finish my projects' not 'I no longer leave my projects unfinished'.

· Make it in the here and now
Write your affirmation in the present tense: 'I finish my projects' rather than 'I will finish my projects'.

· Describe the feeling
Include some positive descriptors, so that you can easily visualize how great it feels to realize your affirmation: 'I finish my projects and I feel so satisfied.'

· Evaluate Does the affirmation you wrote give you a positive feeling? If so, wonderful! You have your affirmation. If not, refine it. You may need a 'stepping stone' to make your affirmation more believable. For example, if you have a complicated track record with finishing what you begin, your subconscious mind may need more help believing 'I finish my projects and I feel so satisfied'. In that case try, 'I believe in the possibility that I finish my projects and feel satisfied', or 'I'm learning to finish my projects with satisfaction and ease'. With time and practice you'll find that you no longer need the stepping stone and you can update your affirmation to 'I easily finish my projects and I'm filled with satisfaction!'

WAYS TO
WORK WITH
CRYSTALS

Crystals are a powerful force as they are but,
in order to optimize their benefits, discover how
to care for and recharge them with regular
cleansing, and learn how to activate them using
the intentions you've developed.

CLEANSE YOUR CRYSTALS

Everything on Earth must go through a process of decay and renewal. Cleansing your crystals can help them reset with a clear energetic frequency. When you cleanse a crystal, imagine that you are clearing it of any energy that it may have picked up from yourself, other people and the environment.

How to Cleanse Your Crystals

Make sure to research your stone to discover if the method you are considering is safe for both you and the crystal. For example, some crystals may dissolve in water or fade in sunlight. Some stones contain trace minerals that may be physically harmful when released into water.

Light: Place your crystal in sunlight or moonlight for an hour.
Salt: Immerse your crystal in salt for about five minutes.
Sound: Chant or use an instrument such as singing bowls, chimes or tuning forks.
Water: Wash your crystal under running water, from a natural water source or a tap, for a few minutes.
Visualization: Imagine crystalline light or archangels surrounding your crystal with the intention of cleansing.
Selenite: Place selenite next to your crystal and leave in place overnight.
Earth: Bury your crystal underground for about a day.

When to cleanse your crystals

It's a good idea to cleanse your crystal when you first get it and about once a month after that. Cleanse more often if you use your crystals regularly.

GROUND
YOURSELF

Before you do any kind of energy work, it's important to get grounded. When a ship puts down its anchor in a quiet harbour, it's protected from being pulled by strong waves back into the sea. As you engage in energy work with crystals, you may drift and dream far afield. It protects you to have an anchor that keeps you connected to the Earth.

How to Get
Grounded

· To begin, set yourself up in a quiet and comfortable space, either seated or lying down. Close your eyes. Imagine that your torso is like a tree trunk with roots growing down through your feet.

· Breathe comfortably and deeply as you imagine your roots flowing down through the ground and all the way to the Earth's core.

· Visualize a healing light moving up through your roots into your body. Imagine this healing light circulating

through your body and carrying any tension or stress away and out, and back down into the Earth.

· Continue to imagine the energy flow – grounding energy coming up through your roots, tension and stress flowing back down to the Earth.

· When you feel relaxed and grounded, give thanks to the Earth before you open your eyes.

ACTIVATE YOUR CRYSTALS

Now that your crystal is cleansed and you are grounded, you can 'program' your crystal with the intention you've developed. Programming your crystal is one way to activate it so that its vibrations are attuned to your desires and goals. It's as simple as telling your crystal what you intend to create or achieve.

How to Program Your Intention

To amplify your crystal's power, focus your thoughts on your intention and train that energy towards your crystal.

- Make sure you have a clear intention or affirmation.

- Set a timer for ten minutes.

- Sit comfortably either in a chair or on the floor.

- Hold your crystal or place it on your body. You could also place it on the floor or on a table in front of you.

- On each inhale, repeat your intention out loud or in your mind.

- On each exhale bring your attention to your crystal.

- When you notice your attention wandering, bring your awareness back to the crystal and your breath.

- Repeat until your timer sounds.

CAPRICORN

DATES: DECEMBER 22–JANUARY 19 ELEMENT: EARTH
MODALITY: CARDINAL PLANET: SATURN SYMBOL: SEA-GOAT
CRYSTAL: GARNET

YOUR SIGN, EXPLAINED

Responsible, accomplished, empowered Capricorn. One of the symbols for your sign is the mountain goat who climbs diligently upwards, motivated by the fresh air and clear view that only exists at the apex of the mountain. The Capricorn motto is 'I establish' – you bring people, resources and ideas together to benefit the collective in tangible ways. Never one to play it small, you establish structures, systems, traditions and institutions that serve many.

Through your work, your dedication and a sense of responsibility, you remind society that we are accountable to those beyond our threshold. The 'sea' part of the 'Sea-goat' symbol adds an emotional texture to your sign as, in astrology, water symbolizes emotions. You put your heart into the work that you do for your family and for your community. You are driven and dedicated.

You make things happen, because you always find yourself in a leadership role. Your communication style is practical and matter-of-fact. Others seek you out for strategies and support. With your measured approach, you are rarely overwhelmed by all this responsibility. And, even if you are, you usually don't show it. A cool customer in emergencies, people count on you to make the right decision on the fly.

Wise beyond your years, you have a mature and sophisticated air about you. This sophistication extends to your taste, which is curated and functional. You look for integrity in all things and are straightforward and sincere.

CAPRICORN IS AN EARTH SIGN

Earth is the physical, the practical, the sensible and sensual. It's the ground beneath your feet. Logical and analytical, you work hard to make the world a better place in measurable, tangible ways.

CAPRICORN IS A TRANSPERSONAL SIGN

Transpersonal signs extend beyond the personal to live and work for the benefit of all people. These signs tend to consider the big picture and can factor other people's feelings and experiences into their own beliefs, goals and dreams.

CAPRICORN IS A CARDINAL SIGN

The cardinal signs correspond to the beginning of each new season. This energy helps Capricorn initiate new projects and enjoy fresh beginnings. Capricorn loves to go first and be a leader.

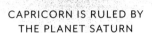

CAPRICORN IS RULED BY THE PLANET SATURN

Saturn symbolizes the tough-love teacher of the zodiac. The ringed planet is making sure you finish your homework and show up to class on time. Through high expectations, Saturn imbues Capricorn with responsibility, resourcefulness and maturity.

THE SEA-GOAT IS THE SYMBOL FOR CAPRICORN

This mythical creature blends qualities of the goat, a resilient animal climbing mountains, with the fish, swimming in depths of emotions. Capricorn is ambitious and feels emotionally responsible for the betterment of society.

GARNET IS A KEY CRYSTAL BIRTHSTONE FOR CAPRICORN

Gleaming burgundy Garnet boosts Capricorn's natural courage, strength and resilience. Choose it as your go-to support when you need to take a risk, follow through on your plans, or boost your energy when your attention wanes. This grounded crystal will help you be true to yourself and your chosen path.

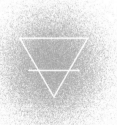

CAPRICORN
TRAITS

Your key traits show how you shine.
These are the special characteristics
that make you unique.

Ambitious   You set your sights high and go after your goals. This level of ambition usually leads to success. Be proud of your many accomplishments.

Strategic   Plan and prepare! With a practical eye to the future, you try never to miss a step or be caught off-guard. Much of your success is down to your knack for strategy.

Patient   You have the capacity to be patient and reassuring. When you're teaching or managing others, you explain things step-by-step, and take a measured approach. However, your trademark patience dissolves when someone is late. Never waste a Capricorn's time!

Traditional   Some Capricorns love holiday traditions that are repeated from year to year. Some find their respect for tradition centres around religion, education, government or societal expectations and customs. You enjoy traditions that reinforce your values.

Exemplary   You have high standards for yourself and others. Personally, you go above and beyond. And you deeply appreciate excellence in the goods and services you invest your time and money in.

Responsible   Reliable is your middle name. When you step up and take responsibility, you feel as if all is right in the world.

Disciplined   Discipline can be a scary word for some people, but you make it look easy. When you create habits and practices that support your goals, you feel as if you're making progress.

Practical   You're down-to-earth, pragmatic and resourceful.

CAPRICORN GIFTS
AND GROWTH AREAS

Your natural gifts offer both strengths and challenges. The same traits that make you special may also require balance at times.

Realistic vs Pessimistic You have a strong sense of reality and you aren't often swayed by idealistic flights of fancy. Sometimes, your rational outlook can cause you to underestimate potential or possibility. Practice being both realistic and hopeful.

Structured vs Stern Enjoy your knack for structure and discipline without becoming inflexible. Rigidity can sap the joy and spontaneity from life. If you're too strict with your routine, you may find that you seem rather stern.

Penny-wise vs Penny-pinching One of your great gifts is that you are an excellent manager of resources. To avoid miserly tendencies, leave room in your budget for generosity.

Focussed vs Fearful Capricorns love to plan! Yes, you can foresee many potential outcomes, and that ability helps you be prepared. But if you start to worry, or overthink things, try to step back and focus on the present moment.

Down-to-earth vs Dry Your practical nature is a grounding anchor for your friends and family. You always have down-to-earth advice. But don't let your sense of realism take over too much. Let loose sometimes and remember to have fun.

Successful vs Stop-at-nothing You're wired for success. Make sure not to let your drive take over your life. Work–life balance is important.

Compatibility is a complex feature of astrology because you are more than just your Sun sign. And other people are multi-faceted too.

Friends

Taurus truly has your back (and since Taurus tends to be hands-on and physical, they might even throw in a backrub if you're lucky)!

Service-oriented **Virgo** will pass you the tools you need when you're up on your ladder of success.

Scorpio digs deep while you think ahead. Together, you've got your bases covered.

Idealistic **Pisces** may seem like a surprising pal for Capricorn, but they know how to bring out your softer side. It's a relief when you can trade in your steadfast realism for **Pisces'** dreamy world.

Foes

Gemini is quick and talkative while yo tend to think carefully before you spea This imbalance may make for some awkward conversations.

Capricorn is mature and ready to work, while **Leo** is childlike and ready to play.

Sagittarius is fired up with possibility, while Capricorn is more interested in probability.

Aquarius pride themselves on disrupting the status quo, while you're more interested in the long-term benefits of tradition and structure.

♉	♏	♊	♐
TAURUS	SCORPIO	GEMINI	SAGITTARI
♍	♓	♌	♒
VIRGO	PISCES	LEO	AQUARIU

CAPRICORN
SUN

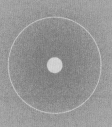

If you were born December 22–January 19, Capricorn is your Sun sign (check your birth chart for an exact calculation). Your Sun sign describes your basic energy.

Just as the Sun is the centre of the solar system, your Sun sign (also called your zodiac sign or star sign) symbolizes the core of your being. As a Capricorn Sun, you deeply value efficiency, organization and leadership. You take things head on, unafraid of conflict and never one to shirk responsibility. You enjoy building, managing, engineering and designing.

At times you may need to soften and slow down. You may benefit from the people and opportunities that remind you to have fun and celebrate your accomplishments. Remember that not everything has to be planned and that your intuition is strong. Let your inner voice guide you to the right choices.

Because your Sun sign fuels your confidence and enlivens your sense of self, there are two recommended crystals for Capricorn Sun. The Amplifying crystal will help you expand upon your gifts and the Balancing crystal will help you integrate your growth areas.

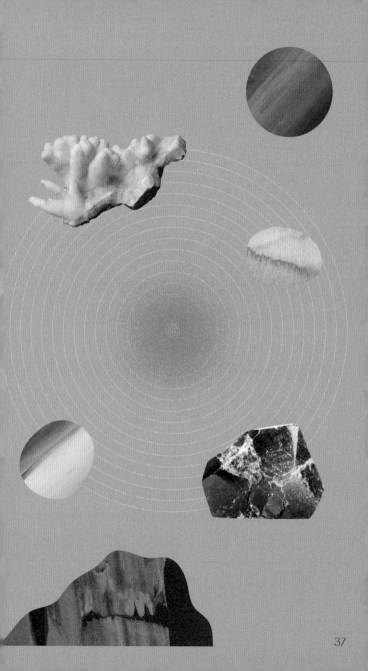

CAPRICORN SUN AMPLIFYING CRYSTAL

STRENGTH, CONSTANCY, STABILITY

Almandine Garnet Reach your full potential with the vitality and courage of Almandine Garnet. The deep maroon flame of this gemstone indicates its subtle fire and grounded strength.

You're good at moving forwards to reach your goals. Almandine Garnet amplifies your Capricorn drive by matching you and then giving you a little extra boost when you need it. This crystal has endurance and may help you stick with your plans when your energy wanes or you yearn to start something new.

Almandine Garnet is a stabilizing stone, and it can support your love of routine and organization. When you need to make practical decisions, take the lead on a project or design a better system, consider carrying down-to-earth Almandine Garnet.

As functional as this crystal is, you may be surprised to learn that it has a soft side, just like earthy Capricorn. This steady stone can fill you with devotion. When you love fully, you are dependable and constant. Almandine Garnet supports your ardour and helps you connect in loving partnership.

CAPRICORN SUN BALANCING CRYSTAL

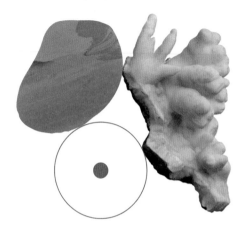

SOOTHING, INTUITION,
OPTIMISM

Blue Aragonite   Here's a cool blue boost for your softer side! Blue Aragonite offers a soothing balm for your emotions. It helps you communicate those tricky feelings. And it gives you courage to name your emotions and talk about them. This cerulean-blue gem has a subtly optimistic and happy vibe. With its gently uplifting qualities, feel empowered to enjoy the flow of your emotions. And, as a bonus, this crystal will help you bravely sit with your feelings – even the challenging ones.

Capricorns tend to be busy people, so you may have a lot on your plate. Let this calming crystal support you emotionally so that you have the internal strength to take on your many responsibilities.

Reach for this sky-blue stone when you want to slow down and open up to your intuition. This emotionally attuned crystal will guide you as you try to listen to your inner voice.

CAPRICORN MOON

SERVICE, NURTURE, PATIENCE

In the same way that the Moon always appears to be changing shape in the sky, the Moon in your chart symbolizes the part of you that is always changing – your emotions.

Imagine that when you have an emotion come up, the Capricorn part of you steps to centre stage. This happens throughout the day. It doesn't matter if the emotion is happiness, sadness, frustration or exhilaration – when emotions arise you go into full Capricorn mode. Your practical, systematic, cautious, deliberate and determined side is accentuated. You focus on planning and your instinct is to make sure that you're prepared.

As a Capricorn Moon, you react with caution. Sometimes, however, emotions can bring out your natural leadership abilities. When spurred by emotion you take charge, make executive decisions, and initiate new projects. You may find that these impulses only last as long as the initial feeling does. A big emotional driver for you is your desire to give back to society. You are motivated to work hard for the betterment of all.

When you get emotional, you try to organize your thoughts and find solid solutions. This tendency makes you an excellent problem-solver, but it can also make you look for problems that aren't there.

You yearn to know that you're on the right track in life. You're most supported by a crystal that helps you feel aligned with your path and purpose.

Ocean Jasper   Ocean Jasper helps you take good care of yourself and others. As a Capricorn Moon, you may tend to put yourself last on the list of your many responsibilities. This speckled, multi-coloured stone can remind you to nurture yourself and slow down.

As a Capricorn Moon, you're already a natural when it comes to helping others in practical ways. Ocean Jasper reminds you how good it feels when you follow your heart and give back to society.

Besides its grounding and nurturing qualities, Ocean Jasper also offers gentle patience, subtle happiness and a confident feeling of being right where you're meant to be.

CAPRICORN RISING

STRENGTH, GROUNDING, HARMONY

Your Rising Sign is the sign that was on the eastern horizon when you were born. It represents the face you show to the world – your social personality. As a Capricorn Rising, you emanate grace and stability. You have a grounded, driven and, at times, serious presence. You tend to prefer a luxurious, elegant look and style.

When it comes to group endeavours, you're a natural fit for the leadership role. You need autonomy and the ability to implement your great ideas and plans. You are competent and reliable. Everyone wants you on their team, because they can tell that you're going places.

Mature beyond your years, you may have been a serious child. Time works in reverse for you, and you seem to become younger at heart as you age.

As a Capricorn Rising, you need a stone that boosts your natural strength and practicality, while at the same time lifting your spirits and helping you take time for yourself.

Smoky Quartz   Smoky Quartz is a tawny-brown, grey or black silicate mineral. This stone of protection and cleansing helps Capricorn Rising in many ways. It amplifies your grounded side and enhances your natural practicality.

When the going gets tough, and something gets you down, reach for Smoky Quartz to help you find harmony and release worries about the future.

A perfect partner for earthy Capricorn, this soothing crystal has a way of boosting your strength when you are feeling overworked or burnt out. Not only that, but this stone supports you in taking life step-by-step, so that you can meet your many goals.

OTHER CAPRICORN SUPPORT CRYSTALS

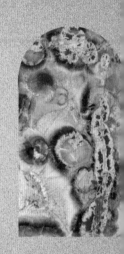

The following crystals are helpful for all Capricorn placements – your Sun, Moon, Rising Sign and any other Capricorn planet or point you may have in your chart. Harness the potential of these stones for clarity and ease in important life areas.

Everyone has different goals for romantic love. In addition, your wishes or desires can change over time. You may wish to attract or pursue love. Perhaps you are hoping to deepen your ability to love, or to open up to intimacy physically, emotionally or spiritually. Love, for Capricorn, feels potent when it reflects your values of growth and progress. You like to take things slow, and you really don't mind being alone. But when you sense that someone would stand by your side in challenging times, your heart softens. You need a crystal ally that can support you in sharing your emotions, healing your heart and increasing your joy.

HEALING
LOVE
SERENITY

Green Tourmaline Experience a renewed feeling of love for yourself and others with the help of Green Tourmaline. This viridian stone's glowing, radiant energy is perfect for the Capricorn who wants to activate the heart and open up to love. A supportive stone, it may help you go with the flow, feel more serenity and even allow you to be more compassionate with yourself. And that sense of compassion can expand in all directions. Allow Green Tourmaline to help amp up your empathy so that you see the best in others. With this crystal by your side, you may feel an overflow of love and joy – and, with it, a sensation of healing.

CAPRICORN × FRIENDSHIP

Friends offer support, fun, love and new perspectives. With Capricorn prominently placed in your chart you might sometimes feel as if you're too busy for a personal life. But we all need the comfort of friendship. You're a truly trustworthy friend. Others count on you for your undying commitment and boundless generosity. When you give advice, it's helpful and practical. You also step up to offer tangible help and service for a friend in need. You have high standards for your friends, and you don't waste your time if someone won't put in the same effort as you do. Integrity and responsibility are key qualities you look for in a friendship.

Yellow Fluorite   Fluorite is excellent for both releasing negativity and stabilizing your sense of self-confidence. This is great for your friendships as it helps you see the bright side of any situation. The Yellow variety of Fluorite has the added benefit of stimulating your mind, your creativity, your conversation skills and your intuition. It's a protective and connecting crystal, allowing you to feel safe, and helping you recognize that you are part of a loving community. If you desire new or deeper friendships, Yellow Fluorite may boost your confidence and conversation skills so that you emerge from your cocoon like a social butterfly.

PROTECTION
STABILITY
CONNECTION

strological insight can help galvanize your money-making potential. Your Capricorn prosperity gifts are leadership, structure, responsibility and planning. If you'd like to make more money, look to these qualities or inspiration. What line of work gives you ots of room to grow and succeed? You thrive hen you feel a sense of ownership and uty, but if you look closely at your budget, ou may find that you are too burdened by xpensive obligations and you might find pportunities for financial freedom. As a Capricorn, your money-management style an be quite organized and structured. You're ne of the best budgeters of the zodiac! If you on't already have a budgeting system, try out ifferent strategies.

**STABILITY
PROSPERITY
CALM**

Tiger's Eye   For support in reaching your prosperity goals, turn to Tiger's Eye. This crystal accentuates your natural money skills – you're practical, perceptive and naturally good at business. Tiger's Eye matches your steady energy, and helps you expand these talents. Tiger's Eye is a striped chalcedony that ranges in hue from shadowy umber to burnished gold. This stabilizing stone can help you make practical and grounded decisions, and its steady energy may also help you calm down and relax if you are worried. Tiger's Eye gives you confidence and serenity so that you can find courage, willpower, or whatever it is you need to keep going, when you're faced with challenges.

Capricorn is the sign that runs the world. You're the leader, go-getter and hard worker of the zodiac. You know how to manage time, people and resources so that your goals are met with efficiency. With a strong respect for tradition, you see yourself as standing on the shoulders of those who went before you. And you are always reaching for higher goals and greater ambitions. In fact, you may get anxious at times of transition and change, so treat yourself with compassion. External validation means a lot to you, so if you aren't in a field of work that offers a traditional system of apprenticeship or promotion, you must create a feeling of accomplishment within yourself.

Clear Quartz Work is your zone of genius, so all you need to do is magnify your natural skills. Clear Quartz is known to be a natural amplifier. Reach for this translucent mineral when you need to concentrate or express your talents more fully. Be deliberate about your goals and intentions and use Clear Quartz to follow through. Clear Quartz is especially helpful with mental focus, so if you are performing a task that demands concentration, you can charge the crystal with your intention and then keep it nearby. This lucid crystal can help you feel clear-headed, so carry it when you want to tune into your intuition, or inspire innovative thinking.

AMPLIFY

FOCUS

INTUITION

Capricorn's symbol is part goat, and you re like this hardy and resilient animal in our sturdy constitution. Even when you do experience setbacks with your health, you tend to figure out a way through, and you aren't afraid to work hard to maintain your well-being. As your sign rules old age, you tend to age well, and you may enjoy a long life. Pay special attention to your bones and joints as Capricorn rules the skeleton. Take precautions to maintain a healthy posture and alignment. A good routine helps you mentally and physically, but learn to be OK with breaking your routine now and then. You enjoy working hard, so burnout may be a problem. Make time for hobbies and pleasurable pursuits.

UPLIFTING
SHIELDING
PROTECTION

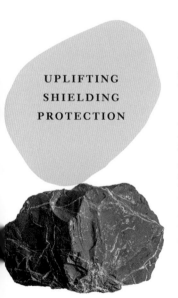

Shungite If you're feeling down or stressed, reach for shiny black Shungite to lift your spirits. This form of carbon is a powerful stone of protection. Some scientific studies have shown it to have anti-bacterial and antioxidant properties. As a Capricorn, you tend to take on a lot of responsibilities, and at times you may feel as if the weight of the world is on your shoulders. This healing stone can help you let go of baggage and feel light-hearted and clear. Shungite may be the perfect aid to help shield your mind from stress and other irritations.

CAPRICORN THROUGHOUT THE YEAR

he energies of the zodiac signs affect us throughout the
ear. In astrology, there is a season for everything. Feeling
eparated from nature's cycles and rhythms can make you
eel out of step or off-kilter. It may add to stress and drain
nergy. Understanding and attuning to astrology's seasons
ight help you feel enlivened.

Take this attunement one step further by using crystals to
mplify the unique energy of each moment, so that you feel
lly aligned with the rhythms of nature.

The following pages take you on a journey with the sun
s it passes through the twelve signs of the zodiac on its
nnual rotation. You will discover the key energies of each
eason, along with a sign-specific horoscope that aligns with
e important themes of your unique chart.

CONFIDENCE AND LEADERSHIP

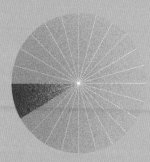

Aries season is the signal that begins the horse race. And they're off! This is the moment to gallop at top speed towards your goals. Put yourself out there with confidence. Make bold decisions and step in time with your intuition. This season is about saying YES to who you are and living your life with freedom. The buds are beginning to emerge and new life is beginning. Sync up with this feeling of potential and possibility.

CAPRICORN HOROSCOPE FOR ARIES SEASON

Connect with important feelings and emotions during Aries season. The Sun is moving through your personal and private world. Themes that come up could relate to your emotional well-being and self-reflection. Or you may be focusing on home, family and ancestors. Give yourself a hug and reach out to those you love.

Morning Practice

Get your heart rate up with
some fiery cardio exercise.

Evening Practice

Cool down that inner
fire with a soothing herbal tea.

CONFIDENCE

Hessonite Garnet   Developing confidence is a practice of
establishing deep self-trust. Let Hessonite Garnet's activating
and powerful energy help you build up your courage so that
you can just go for it. Also try Green Aventurine, Orange
Calcite or Malachite.

LIVING BOLDLY

Pink Aventurine   When the time is ripe for taking bold
action, Pink Aventurine can help you advance into your next
adventure. Reach for it when you need a boost of fun. This
spirited crystal connects you with your heart centre, and acts
as your best accomplice in bravery and boldness. Or choose
Ruby, Tangerine Quartz or Sardonyx.

DRIVE

Fire Agate   Aries season is the vehicle in which to follow
your passions and desires, which makes Fire Agate the
gasoline. Whether you need to get an important project
going or just tackle spring cleaning, put yourself on track to
get things done by syncing up with the vibration of this fierce
crystal. You could also reach for Bloodstone, Stromatolite
or Cinabrite.

MONEY AND
SELF-WORTH

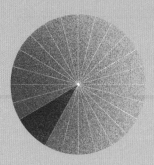

Like working in a garden and then enjoying the beauty that you've cultivated, Taurus represents sustained effort that leads to a productive reward. This season is the prime time to focus on building up your sense of personal worth and value. On one level, this process may involve nurturing your self-esteem. On another level, this may include thinking about security, money and finances. Taurus season is also a time to remember the beauty of life. It reminds us that no matter what is going on, there are simple pleasures to be had.

CAPRICORN HOROSCOPE
FOR TAURUS SEASON

Appreciate your creative side. So much of life is spent being productive, right now it's time to just be yourself! Enjoy yourself, admire the beauty of nature and take creative action. Give yourself the freedom to enjoy being alive. Shine bright like the Sun and be recognized for your unique qualities.

Morning Practice

Practice gratitude by reminding
yourself of three things you're
grateful for.

Evening Practice

Do something that feels good to
your body, like stretching or
wearing soft clothing.

CRYSTALS FOR
TAURUS SEASON

MONEY MAGIC

Green Jade   No matter where you are beginning
financially, Green Jade will juice up your money situation.
This abundance stone has a way of amplifying your potential.
A soft and expansive prosperity stone that soothes the spirit, it
will support you as you make wise financial decisions. Reach
for it when you crave a feeling of security. You could also use
Pyrite, Emerald or Epidote.

SELF-WORTH

Red Jasper   Red Jasper will amp up your self-appreciation
quotient. Choose Red Jasper when you're feeling uncertain, if
your confidence could use a boost, or if you want to feel more
resilient in any way. This stone will get you in the groove of
trusting your own value. Also try Carnelian, Chrysocolla or
Bixbite.

ABUNDANCE

Green Apatite   If you are feeling like something in your life
is lacking, such as money, time, energy, sleep, or support, for
example, you might need to boost your sense of abundance.
Taurus season is the perfect time to grasp hold of that feeling
of nature's plentifulness. Use Green Apatite to replenish your
energy and help you feel satisfied and satiated with what you
have. You could also reach for Golden Tourmaline, Uvarovite
Garnet or Agate.

VALUES
AND COMMUNITY

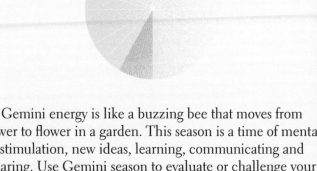

Gemini energy is like a buzzing bee that moves from flower to flower in a garden. This season is a time of mental stimulation, new ideas, learning, communicating and sharing. Use Gemini season to evaluate or challenge your mindset and values. Which attitudes are no longer serving you? What's truly important to you? Gemini season is also a time to connect with others in the community. What can you learn from others? What can you teach others? It's a fun and lively season full of new connections.

CAPRICORN HOROSCOPE
FOR GEMINI SEASON

Attend to the important details of life. The Sun is traversing your sector of organization, health and responsibilities. It's a great time to be proactive, use your natural planning skills to think ahead, and create healthy new habits. This is an excellent season to reorganize and rethink your space, workflow, nutrition and schedule.

Morning Practice	Evening Practice
Help a new mindset emerge with a potent Gemini season intention.	Before falling asleep, envision yourself having a great time at a party surrounded by everyone you love.

CRYSTALS FOR GEMINI SEASON

MASTER YOUR MINDSET

Heliodor   Have repeating thoughts, fears or anxieties been plaguing you? Use the revitalizing energy of Gemini season and Heliodor to hit the reset button on these old thought patterns. This stone will gently help you harmonize your thoughts and adjust your mindset, helping you reconnect with your true values. Alternatively, try Blue Lace Agate, Chrome Chalcedony or Dragonstone.

CONNECTING

Agatized Coral   When you really want to feel connected, seen, heard and understood, reach for Agatized Coral. This fossilized coral nudges you to reach out to others and helps you analyse your relationships, whether with friends, lovers, family, neighbours or colleagues. It relays an upbeat feeling so that you can view your relationships with the people in your life with optimism. You may also choose Citrine, Apricot Agate or Bismuth.

COMMUNICATION

Aquamarine   Aquamarine is your crystal-clear communication companion. Communication helps us feel connected, and allows us to learn and grow. In those moments when you feel confused or foggy, this elegant stone will help you become grounded and steady. Use Aquamarine to find your voice – it will help you tune into your own true message and the truth of those around you. Alternatively, reach for Turquoise, Prairie Tanzanite or Green Chrysocolla.

HOME AND NURTURE

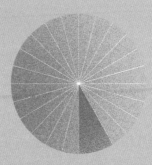

Come on home to Cancer season. Like Cancer's symbol, the Crab, wrap yourself in a protective shell and reflect on your life and your feelings. In Cancer season, engage in meaningful self-care, and also put your energy into nurturing others. Discover what makes you feel safe and cosy. This could be your actual home, your closest relationships or tending to the feelings and needs of your inner child.

CAPRICORN HOROSCOPE FOR CANCER SEASON

With the Sun moving through your area of relationships, you might find yourself focusing on your most important partnerships. This could include life partners, business partners, or anyone with whom you share a special bond. It might be time to have a heart-to-heart conversation, clear the air, or redefine your expectations of a relationship. Pay special attention to the people who really matter.

Affirmation
I NURTURE MYSELF AND ACCEPT MYSELF JUST AS I AM.

Morning Practice	Evening Practice
Let your inner child take the lead: what do they want to do today?	Sing a lullaby to soothe your inner child before bed.

CRYSTALS FOR CANCER SEASON

NURTURING

Blue Calcite   What do you want to actively care for? Yourself? A child? A creative project? In order to feel truly nurturing, you need to feel inspired by love. Blue Calcite will help you soften and open up your heart centre, so that you feel drawn to put your compassionate and attentive energy where it is needed most. Other nurturing crystals include Moonstone, Blue Chalcedony and Bumblebee Jasper.

HOME ENVIRONMENT

Pink Mangano Calcite   Home is where you are safe and protected. It's your emotional nest where you can relax. Use Pink Mangano Calcite to create a grounded and peaceful home environment. This stone acts as a balm that will help you feel harmonized. Place this rosy crystal in your inner sanctum and set the intention to soothe conflict and soften your environment so that you can restore your energy after a long day or week. You could also try Chiastolite, Rose Quartz or Peach Moonstone.

FAMILY BONDS

Bornite   Family, whether chosen or blood-related, represent some of our closest relationships. Use Bornite to foster the strength of family relationships. This is a joyful stone that will help you embrace the positives that come from your family circle, while at the same time grounding you to help you remember who you are as an individual. Also try Orange Calcite, Indigo Gabbro or Girasol Quartz.

CREATIVITY AND FUN

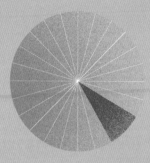

Harnessing your creativity and expressing your true self with others, that's the key to making the most of Leo season. It's all about playful sharing and creative shining. Radiate your magnificent heart of gold outwards with immediacy, freedom, spontaneity, generosity and a giant sense of fun. During this season of wholehearted self-expression, take a little time to remember how unique you are. Remember what inspires you and reflect on what you love most about yourself.

CAPRICORN HOROSCOPE FOR LEO SEASON

This is a transformative phase, as you let something old fall away and welcome in a fresh beginning. Be tender and gentle with yourself through this process. The thing that is changing may be monumental, or relatively insignificant. Regardless, take your time and feel the feelings that come up around letting go. New realizations are percolating beneath the surface.

Morning Practice

Create daily.

Evening Practice

Seek out a chance to laugh every
day and go to bed with a smile on
your face.

CRYSTALS FOR
LEO SEASON

INSPIRATION

Rutilated Quartz   Inspiration is the creative spark and
Rutilated Quartz can help you turn that spark into a roaring
bonfire. Make Leo season feel lit up with creativity. Keep
Rutilated Quartz by your side when you need an inventive
solution to a problem at work, when your love life could use
an inspiring reboot, or when you are ready to awaken the artist
within. Set your intentions and let this highly programmable
stone carry the flame of your dreams. You could also use
Sunstone, Golden Labradorite or Yellow Sapphire.

SELF-APPRECIATION

Thulite   Leo season is the time to shed all insecurities and
put your faith in your one true self. Loving yourself dissolves
insecurity and self-criticism. Thulite tunes you into the
vibration of love, peace and harmony, allowing you to be
present and wholly yourself. Alternatively, reach for Ruby,
Larimar, or Desert Jasper.

COURAGE

Golden Apatite   To ensure your lion-heartedness knows no
bounds, you need to fire up your courage. Golden Apatite
bestows upon you both passion and discernment, which
determine which fears are baseless. Use it when you need
to take a risk at work, strike up a conversation with someone
you admire or stand up for your values. Other courage-giving
crystals are Carnelian, Iolite-Sunstone or Citrine.

HEALTH
AND HABITS

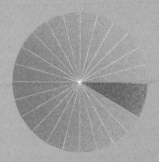

Our goals and dreams require a big-picture view,
but Virgo season reminds us that life is actually lived in the
small details. Focus on how you are living your life, your
everyday routines and rituals. On a practical level, what is
important to you? Virgo energy helps you take a closer
look at your health and habits, and how you can be
of service to others as well.

CAPRICORN HOROSCOPE
FOR VIRGO SEASON

This is your moment to break the mould.
The Sun is moving through your zone
of expansion, so break free and open
your mind. You may well connect with
a new value or ideal that inspires you to
take your life in a new direction. Or you
may take a trip that gets you out of your
comfort zone and encourages you to
expand your perspective. Enjoy feeling
invigorated and alive.

Morning Practice	**Evening Practice**
Drink a glass of water first thing.	Write down one task you're going to complete tomorrow, and stick to it.

CRYSTALS FOR VIRGO SEASON

FOCUS

Clear Quartz   Virgo season ushers in a chance to notice the details and get focused. Use Clear Quartz to take you all the way there. This cleansing stone helps you rivet your attention on your commitments. When you program Clear Quartz with your intention for focus, you'll find that it supports you, whether you have a tight deadline or you just really need to concentrate. You could also turn to Vanadinite, Amazonite or Tiger Iron.

HEALTH

Chevron Amethyst   A lot of factors go into maintaining optimum health: genetics, diet, exercise, access to care, to name just a few. Virgo season energy will encourage you to think wisely about the preventative measures that you can take to boost both your mental well-being and physical health. Use Chevron Amethyst for gentle motivation that can help you happily embrace healthier choices. Or try Girasol Quartz, Ruby Fuchsite or Black Tourmaline.

ALTRUISM

Stromatolite   Humanity wouldn't be a successful species without the desire to be of service to others. Virgo season plus Stromatolite is your recommendation for kindness and selfless action. Turn your attention to what you can do to help others, whether that's volunteering, making a donation to a good cause, or simply smiling and being friendly. Let Stromatolite amplify your altruistic nature. Alternatively, reach for Stichtite, Rhodonite or Rose Quartz.

61

RELATIONSHIPS AND BALANCE

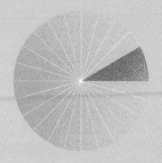

Libra season is symbolized by balanced scales.
It's a chance to look at all life areas and judge the
equilibrium. Are your relationships in balance? Do both
people in your relationships have what they want and
need? This can be a fun and harmonious time to socialize.
During Libra season, balance can also be created in your
environment through art, decoration and organization.
The scales are the symbol for justice and Libra season bring
a collective yearning to make the systems of government
more fair and to expose inequalities.

CAPRICORN HOROSCOPE FOR LIBRA SEASON

The focus is on work, career and
vocation. These are some of Capricorn's
favourite topics! The time is ripe for
planning, setting new goals and gaining
recognition in your field. You may feel
driven to work hard and achieve. Be
strategic and trust in yourself. You have
the skills that you need to be a success.

Affirmation
BALANCE EXISTS IN ALL AREAS OF MY LIFE.

Morning Practice	Evening Practice
Reach out and message someone who is important to you, and tell them why.	Meditate to create mental balance.

HEALTHY BOUNDARIES

Iolite   Communicating what you want, need and desire is a great starting point to gain clarity in your relationships. Iolite can help you reflect and get to know yourself – the first step to speaking and sharing your truth with others. Once your inner base is stabilized, Iolite can help you reach out to another person, while maintaining your own healthy boundaries. This healing stone has a peaceful energy that helps you create balance between yourself and a partner. You could also use Amazonite, Purple Jade or Chiastolite.

BALANCE

Shungite   Balance is an active state, requiring constant adjustment. It comes under the jurisdiction of the intellectual, analytical sign of Libra. Keep checking in with yourself throughout Libra season to determine what needs more balance. For a crystal that will help you stay steady, reach for Shungite. Or choose Diopside, Selenite or Turquoise.

DECISIVENESS

Ametrine   Libra season is an excellent time to analyse, think things through and come up with new ideas. Keep Ametrine by your desk for productive planning sessions and for when you have big decisions to make. This balancing stone will help you keep your life on track. As an alternative, try Variscite, Fluorite or White Sapphire.

TRANSFORMATION
AND FORGIVENESS

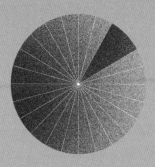

Scorpio season pulls you deeper – emotionally, physically and spiritually. This is a season of transformation, helping you to feel deeply, release old emotions and thought patterns, and get ready to move on to the next stage. By pulling back the layers and being honest with the truth of who you are, it's also an opportunity to deepen your relationships with others by letting them get to know the real you.

CAPRICORN HOROSCOPE
FOR SCORPIO SEASON

Set your sights on the future. What is your vision? Who do you want by your side? Imagining and envisioning your dreams can feel fun and freeing. The Sun is moving through your zone of hopes, dreams and wishes for the future. Pay special attention to your desires for your community. What world will you create?

Morning Practice

Forgive yourself
for something.

Evening Practice

Forgive someone else
for something.

CRYSTALS FOR
SCORPIO SEASON

INTIMACY

Red Tourmaline   Scorpio season propels you to create
warmth and closeness. But opening yourself up to the
vulnerability of intimacy demands courage. Whether you are
setting the stage for sexual intimacy or emotional intimacy,
Red Tourmaline will help you feel confident enough to
embrace deep connection with others. Other crystals for
intimacy are Garnet, Shiva Lingam or Red Aventurine.

TRANSFORMATION

Moldavite   Transformation brings both endings and
new beginnings. Moldavite will help you spiritually and
emotionally adjust when change comes into your life – when
a relationship has run its course, a shift is needed in the
work arena or a new adventure calls your name. When the
transformation you are undergoing is more subtle in texture,
like saying goodbye to an old habit, Moldavite will help you
align with your new reality. Or try Shungite, Moss Agate
or Tugtupite.

FORGIVENESS

Dioptase   Whether you need to be kinder to yourself or let go
of hurt that someone else has caused you, forgiveness doesn't
happen all at once. It's a process that you set in motion. Finding
forgiveness requires self-love, self-worth and understanding.
Dioptase can help you practice forgiveness by supporting you
with its gentle and loving vibrations. You could also turn to
Black Moonstone, Rhodochrosite or Pink Tourmaline.

WISDOM
AND FREEDOM

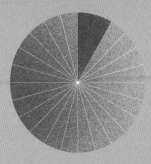

Sagittarius season is represented by the archer who shoots high and blazes a trail into new territory. The archer is also a centaur – half horse and half human, half wild and half philosophical. Sagittarius season is a time to feel fiercely alive and simultaneously inspired to ask big, existential questions. It's a season for expanding your boundaries and traveling physically and mentally to understand more about the world and the human experience.

CAPRICORN HOROSCOPE
FOR SAGITTARIUS SEASON

The universe is calling you to retreat and restore. Take some time out to get to know yourself once again. Connect with your heart and your true self. Let the feelings flow. During busy times, we don't always have time to honour our feelings and the changes that are occurring in our lives. Now is your season to slow down and connect with your emotions.

Affirmation

I TRUST MY INNER WISDOM.

Morning Practice

Go for a walk or
a jog out in nature.

Evening Practice

Memorize an
inspiring quote.

INNER WISDOM

Azurite   In Sagittarius season, the archer knows that the best
way to take aim is to trust your inner wisdom. When you are
connected to your true self, it's easier to make choices. Life
feels more satisfying. Azurite is the stone to hold and carry
when you want to bolster your self-confidence and tune into
your wisdom. Or choose Idocrase, Shattuckite or Amethyst.

EXPANSION

Jasper   Ruled by the gas giant Jupiter, Sagittarius is the
sign of expansion. During this season, you can move beyond
anything that is limiting you. Is there an area of your life in
which you feel trapped in a cage? Maybe if you take a closer
look, you'll find that the door to the cage has been open the
entire time. Feel the freedom and expansion that is available
to you with the help of Jasper. This enlivening stone will help
you break out into new territory. Alternatives are Blue Topaz,
Pink Chalcedony or Ruby Iolite.

ADVENTURE AND TRAVEL

Turquoise   When you're setting out in search of new
horizons, reach for Turquoise as your talisman for protection
and luck. Travel and adventure require equal parts bravery
and boldness, but the reward is an expanded mindset and
perspective. Let Turquoise be your steady support system as
you push beyond your boundaries to discover excitement,
new opportunity and enlightenment. You could also use
Green Opal, Smoky Quartz or Aventurine.

CAREER
AND GOALS

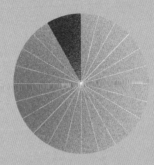

Like the mountain goat, in Capricorn season
you are primed to choose your footing carefully as
you make your ascent. Capricorn season brings practical
and productive forward motion. Use this energy efficiently
and tactically. You may choose to counterbalance this drive
and ambition with a large dose of acceptance, both
of yourself and others. Remember to give yourself a
break; you are trying your best.

CAPRICORN HOROSCOPE
FOR CAPRICORN SEASON

This is your special season, dear
Capricorn! Put yourself out there
and enjoy some attention. Make your
mark on the world. Let the unique
parts of your personality shine brightly.

Because you're such a practical person
others may seek you out for advice and
support. Say yes to these requests only
when you feel inspired. This is your
moment to put yourself first.

**EVERY DAY, IN EVERY WAY,
I AM GETTING BETTER.**

Morning Practice

Write down your goals.

Evening Practice

Reflect on your
accomplishments.

ACHIEVEMENT

Fluorite   Your Capricorn season recommendation supports
you in taking things one step at a time while staying focused
on your big picture goals. Look to Fluorite. Fluorite's unique
vibration can help you concentrate, while energizing you so
that you can keep moving forwards. Or look for support from
Ocean Jasper, Septarian Nodule or Tiger's Eye.

CAREER

Cat's Eye   Capricorn season is a wonderful time to take
stock. While you think about your work life, keep Cat's Eye by
your side. This stone helps you know your strengths, which is
imperative for a fulfilling career. It will help you feel optimistic
and believe in yourself. Cat's Eye's structured energy helps
you know your personal boundaries and make smart money
choices. You could also use Andradite Garnet, Apatite or
Hawk's Eye.

FOR SELF-ACCEPTANCE

Blue Aragonite   Let calming Blue Aragonite guide you
when you need to feel the soothing balm of self-acceptance.
Capricorn season pushes you to achieve, which may cause
you to question your progress in life. Counterbalance that by
learning to accept yourself for who you are. Blue Aragonite
has a compassionate energy that may inspire you to be less
judgemental towards yourself and show yourself more kindness.
Other crystals for self-acceptance are Prasiolite, Amethyst
or Shungite.

FRIENDSHIP AND VISION

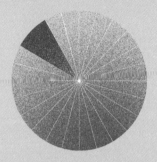

Aquarius season pushes people and ideas to the forefront. What are your big ideas for the future? And who is in your community? Your vision for the future may also be a vision for humanity. Take the time to research causes to which you might contribute time, money and resources. Your friends, communities and social groups are extra important during this season, so prioritize the people who mean the most to you.

CAPRICORN HOROSCOPE FOR AQUARIUS SEASON

The practical side of your personality is boosted right now. As the Sun moves through your zone of money and resources, your attention is drawn towards matters of security. During this season, you are fascinated with your financial condition so you may enjoy budgeting and planning for your future. Discover what helps you feel safe and secure.

Morning Practice

~reate a vision board and make it the
~st thing you see when you wake up.

Evening Practice

Call a friend for a
meaningful chat.

CRYSTALS FOR
AQUARIUS SEASON

FRIENDSHIP

Bismuth   Aquarius season asks you to turn towards your
community. What can you offer? What will you receive?
Friends enrich your life in so many ways, but mostly by
encouraging your feeling of belonging – a natural mood
booster. Bismuth has an expansive energy that helps you join
with others in a shared sense of community. Carry Bismuth as a
reminder that you are connected to others. Or you could reach
for Carnelian, Sunset Sodalite or Blue Apatite.

FAITH IN THE FUTURE

Cavansite   The future is uncertain. Sometimes you need a
boost to help you trust in the potential and possibility of what
the future can become. In that case, reach for Cavansite.
This stone has a sweet vibe of positivity that can give you the
courage to believe in your biggest dreams for the future. Some
alternatives are Peridot, Muscovite or Auralite 23.

VIBRATIONAL LIFT

Apophyllite   When Aquarius season asks you to turn
your attention to what is possible, it helps to have a positive
outlook. Without suppressing any challenging feelings (those
are important and need to be processed), pay some special
attention to the positive things in your life and work to create
an enduring, positive mindset. If you need a little extra support,
reach for Clear or Green Apophyllite. This high-vibe crystal
can lift your spirits and help you feel full of potential. You
could also try Quartz, Hematite or Angelite.

INTUITION AND SPIRITUALITY

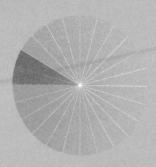

The most mystical season of all, Pisces season is the time to tune into your intuition. Slide like a slippery fish into the sphere of your dreams, faith, spirituality, compassion and creativity. This is a moment to rest, reflect and look inwards. Reconnect with your imagination. Feel your feelings. Plug into your spirituality or whatever makes you feel connected to the universe.

CAPRICORN HOROSCOPE FOR PISCES SEASON

You're ready to expand your mind and enliven your friendships. With the Sun moving through your zone of mental and social connections, you may feel a buzzy excitement to get out there and mingle. New people can bring you new ideas. New ideas can inspire you. This is your season to write, journal, talk, teach, learn and share with others.

Morning Practice

Record your dreams.

Evening Practice

Do some freewriting
to clear your mind.

CRYSTALS FOR
PISCES SEASON

COMPASSION

Lavender Quartz   Lavender Quartz helps you feel peace and
understanding for others. It will bestow upon you the softness
that you need to open up to other people's perspectives. It will
also allow you to dissolve drama with a heightened sense of
empathy. This soothing and healing stone can offer strength
while you stand in someone else's shoes. A compassionate life
is a fulfilling life. As an alternative, turn to Thulite, Prehnite
with Epidote or Fluorite.

INTUITION

Pink Opal   When you trust your inner guidance system you
have ultimate clarity. Harness the power of your intuition
in Pisces season with the help of Pink Opal. This stone will
help you connect to yourself and to your guides. It raises
the volume on your inner 'Yes' or 'No' by quietening any
distractions and helping you connect within. Other crystals
for intuition are Clear Quartz, Moldavite or Dumortierite.

FOR FAITH

Celestite   Faith can be thought of as a complete trust or
confidence in someone or something. With a little bit of
faith you may find it easier to contend with fear or anxiety.
But trust and faith must be developed from within. In Pisces
season, harness the power of high-vibrational Celestite to
help you move beyond unnecessary fears as you put your
trust in something bigger. You could also use Vatican Stone,
Apophyllite or Turquoise.

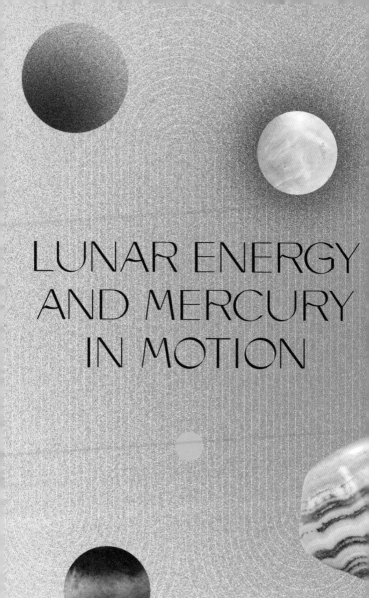

LUNAR ENERGY AND MERCURY IN MOTION

THE LUNAR
CYCLE

In astrology, the Moon is a catalyst, helping us to move forwards with our goals and intentions.

The 29-day lunar cycle begins in darkness. The Moon then appears as a faint crescent and grows bigger until it's full. This process, from darkness to Full Moon, mirrors the incubation and development of your own creative process. Then, the Moon wanes until it completely disappears, reflecting another stage of the creative cycle – the process of releasing your efforts and making space for another cycle to begin. This allows new thoughts and ideas to emerge.

Each of the eight phases of the Moon cycle offers a different type of energy, which we will explore in this chapter. You can follow the Moon through the lunar month with crystal recommendations, setting your intentions in alignment with the New Moon and letting the lunar cycle help you make that intention into reality. The lunar cycle will also help you cleanse and release so that you can gently transition into the next phase.

By using crystals to work with the lunar cycle you can activate the potential of the Moon and amplify its energy. Through visualization or meditation, tap into the unique energies of each stage of the Moon cycle with the following crystals. For the suggested rituals at each phase, choose a crystal from the recommended options, or substitute with your favourite crystal.

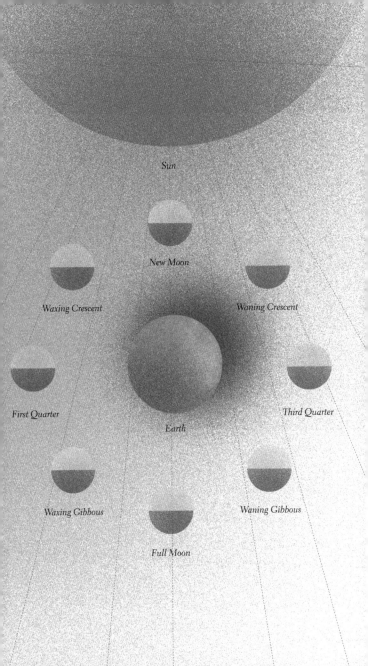

SET YOUR NEW INTENTIONS

The Moon is dark. This is a time for reflection and a time to connect with your inner self. Use your energy to envision what you would like to make happen. What do you desire? What are your dreams? Anything is possible – imagine that you are planting seeds of intention that will manifest and grow throughout the Waxing Moon Phase. The New Moon is a quiet and emotional time and you may discover that, as you think about what you would like to create, many different feelings arise. Excitement, anticipation, fear, worry – whatever feelings arise, make space for those feelings and be gentle with yourself. Listen to your intuition and imagine your next steps.

Black Moonstone can support you during the delicate and sensitive New Moon vibration. It offers wellsprings of patience and peace as you work with your emotions and reflect on your life. When your dreams are germinating under the surface, Black Moonstone can help you trust your own process.

Labradorite opens your third eye wide so that you can tune into your intuition and design your goals in accordance with your path and purpose.

Pink Sapphire's loving energy can buffer you and help you feel emotionally at ease.

Ametrine provides sweet joy and concentrated focus so that you can set intentions with confidence.

TRUST,
INSPIRATION, SERENITY
AND DELIGHT

New Moon Ritual

Freewrite about what you yearn for and anything else that's on your mind. Then jot down your intentions for this Moon cycle on a piece of paper and place your chosen crystal on top.

NURTURE YOUR INTENTIONS

our seeds of intention are germinating
under the soil, and maybe some of the
plants are just beginning to sprout. As
the lunar energy builds momentum,
make sure that you have the resources
you need to achieve your goals. Provide
structure and support for yourself. This
cycle is just beginning to take shape,
so consider how your choices will
determine your direction – maybe there
are changes you'd like to make to your
goals. Remain curious throughout this
process, because anything is possible!

Turquoise is a powerhouse of a
crystal that can deftly carry you
through the precarious Waxing
Crescent phase. At this moment
you need a subtle combination of
confidence, discernment, curiosity and
commitment. Turquoise can help you
understand the truth of what you need
to create, and it can help you stay open
and accepting of your process. Use this
stone as you decide what you really
want to manifest and commit to during
this Moon cycle.

Shattuckite helps you intuitively
illuminate your path so that you can
make the decisions that are right for you.

Pyrite offers crystalline protection
and is a wonderful choice to help you
realize your goals.

Orange Calcite gives you mental focus
and lots of energy for the journey ahead.

TRUTH,
INTUITION, MANIFESTATION
AND FOCUS

Waxing Crescent Moon Ritual

Read and rewrite your intentions for this Moon cycle.
Decorate the paper and place your chosen crystal back on top.

BUILD YOUR MOMENTUM

Look around your garden of intentions and discover what is growing. Have your goals started to take shape? If so, how are they coming along? Do you need more support? Perhaps you have had surprising results? At the First Quarter Moon the constraints of reality can be intimidating. You have big dreams, but sometimes you encounter resistance when dreams make contact with real world limitations. Maybe there is more work required than you had foreseen, or there are real-world issues with time, money, support or other resources. Give yourself lots of encouragement. Pivot, and reassess if necessary. This is an exciting, high energy time, so keep taking action and building momentum.

Bumblebee Jasper When reality, and all of its limitations, hits, Bumblebee Jasper can help you stay the course with confidence. Lean on this crystal when you need the energy to just keep moving forwards. It will subdue your fears and inspire you to push past your comfort zone.

Peridot is a cheery companion that will help you look at any situation with optimism.

Tangerine Quartz offers creative potential that makes problem solving effortless.

Aventurine will vitalize you and give you the confidence to keep going.

CONFIDENCE,
OPTIMISM, CREATIVITY AND
VITALITY

First Quarter Moon Ritual

Light a candle, hold your chosen crystal and
visualize your intentions being realized.

DEVELOP YOUR INTENTIONS

's astonishing what a little effort can reate! Now that you've made it to the Vaxing Gibbous phase of the Moon ycle, you are starting to see the effects f the intentions that you set. If your oal was to improve your nutrition, you nay be feeling better already. If you elt motivated to get out there and start ating, you may have started some new onversations. Whatever the last few ays have revealed, now is the time to oll up your sleeves and actively give nape to your garden. What will you eed out? What is working, and what n't working? What changes might you nake? The intensity has almost peaked o take tender care of your emotional ell-being as you keep putting in effort owards your dreams.

Jet Jet's grounding energy will help you establish deep root systems for your developing intentions. When you need strength and motivation to keep pushing forwards with your goals, this stone will support you. As a bonus, jet has a sheltering vibration that can steady you emotionally and help you surge forwards with optimism and hope.

Hematite offers balance and protection, helping you proactively take care of yourself during this active time.

Carnelian lights your fire with sparkling enthusiasm and convinces you to tune into your creative side.

Blue Lace Agate calms your mind, allowing you to weed through your options and make solid decisions.

GROUNDING,
PROTECTION, ENTHUSIASM
AND PEACE OF MIND

Waxing Gibbous Moon Ritual

While holding or wearing your chosen crystal, do something that feels active or expressive, such as dancing, painting, gardening, cooking or singing. Imagine your goals and repeat your intentions.

81

HARVEST

Everything is revealed under the light of the Moon. The attempts you've made, your wins, your losses. It's time to get out in the garden and harvest the crop. Regardless of whether the bounty lives up to your expectations, there is something to appreciate and celebrate. At the Full Moon, honour what you've created and give gratitude to yourself for your commitment. This phase represents the push and pull of two opposite energies as the Moon is in the opposite sign to the Sun. The result is a highly polarized and intense energy that can heighten emotions, pull you in two different directions, or cause you to realize something important. Make sure to be very gentle with yourself and those around you.

EMOTIONAL EXPLORATION, ABUNDANCE, PEACEFULNESS AND RECEPTIVITY

White Moonstone symbolizes the Full Moon and all of its glorious creativity and excitement. This pearly white crystal shines a bright light so that you can see clearly. As you examine the fruits that you've cultivated during the Waxing Moon phase, use the receptive and healing energy of White Moonstone to help you accept and celebrate. It's time for gratitude, and this comforting crystal will help you open up to that feeling.

Green Apatite is an antidote to the drama of the Full Moon – use it to highlight joy and abundance.

Jade has a subtle, soothing energy that imparts an optimistic attitude.

Stilbite connects the heart, mind and intuition – this can help you rationally balance your emotions while still opening up to divine insight.

Full Moon Ritual

Hold your chosen crystal and write down three things that you are grateful for. The Full Moon is also a great time to cleanse your crystals. Place them outside or on a windowsill and let them bathe in the Moon's healing energy.

REFLECT AND REVIEW

Now that the intensity of the full reveal has begun to wane, you can settle deeper into your new reality. Indulge yourself and enjoy. As the Moon has moved through waxing to waning, this is the beginning of a less active and more receptive phase. This means that you can simply sit with the ebbing fullness of what is. Begin a process of compassionate review. What have you learned? What will you do differently in the next Moon cycle? Each lunar cycle reveals an older, more experienced version of who you are becoming. So sink into this moment of reflection and get to know yourself once more.

Obsidian offers a protective energy that buffers and supports. Use it at the Waning Gibbous phase of the Moon cycle to release the past and securely recline into the experience of the moment. Obsidian's cleansing vibes can help you remove any junk from your thought patterns, allowing you to think from a new perspective. Harness its clarifying energy to appraise your situation with equanimity and objectivity.

Tiger's Eye is for encouragement and strength as you review your progress and make plans for improvement.

Citrine offers joy and optimism so that you can look at your accomplishments through a positive lens.

Celestite provides tranquillity as you come down off the high of the Full Moon.

PROTECTION,
STRENGTH, JOY AND
TRANQUILLITY

Waning Gibbous Moon Ritual

Pour yourself some tea, water, or other drink of your choice, and take the time to sit and quietly appreciate the moment. With your chosen crystal nearby, review your intention and gratitude lists.

LET GO

Get comfortable letting go so that you can make space for new things. At the Last Quarter Moon allow the leaves to fall and the fading plants to return to the soil. A tree drops its leaves to conserve resources. Take stock of what you want to let go of, so that you can use your energy wisely. Is there someone you need to forgive? Do you need to release your expectations and accept something about your life? Release the past or an outdated way of thinking, let go and forgive. Maybe you declutter your closet, acknowledge your reality, admit your mistakes, get really honest with yourself, or forgive yourself or others. The Last Quarter Moon asks that you put in a little effort to let go of the emotions and ideas that are taking up excess energy.

**LOVE, SUPPORT,
GROUNDING AND GENTLE
SELF-REFLECTION**

Rose Quartz is an emotional balm that can help you forgive yourself and others. As the Last Quarter Moon inspires you to release your expectations and accept your current reality, you need a soothing support that helps you open up compassionately. Rose Quartz brings playful, loving vibes and helps you gently accept a situation and move forwards.

Rutilated Quartz offers a powerful support in following through on your intentions as you review what you've learned and plan for the next phase.

Smoky Quartz provides grounding, protection and assistance in clearing the thoughts and feelings that you are ready to release.

Amethyst is for gently releasing old mental patterns and contemplating new possibilities.

Last Quarter Moon Ritual

Create a peaceful environment and run a bath for yourself. Place a water-safe, non-toxic crystal (such as Quartz or Amethyst) in the bath while you review your intentions from this moon cycle. Repeat these affirmations, 'I make space for clarity' and 'I release the past'.

STILLNESS AND REST

The lunar energy is encouraging you to turn inwards and be still. All is quiet in the winter of your metaphorical garden. Embracing stillness offers many benefits. By allowing your inner landscape to exist without judgement, you honour who you are now. Slowing down can also help you uncover your values and emotional truth – which may not be so apparent when you are busily running around. And last but not least, rest and quiet will help you recharge your energy for the next cycle. Challenge yourself to slow down and be present in the moment. There will be ample time for new plans and dreams when the next cycle begins.

Serpentine can help you open a gateway to the stillness within and to the profound interconnectedness of the universe. Using this crystal during your Waning Crescent Moon meditations will help you feel buffered and supported in the understanding that there is no-one you need to be and nothing you need to do. Float along with the waves of existence. You'll know when the time is right again for action.

Selenite radiates cleansing energy that can help you release the past cycle and prepare to make a fresh start.

Howlite soothes your spirit and quietens any absurd complaints from your 'inner critic'.

Aquamarine helps you create a meditative state of mind so that you can listen to the stillness within.

CONNECTION WITH
NATURE, CLEANSING,
SOOTHING AND REFLECTION

Waning Crescent Moon Ritual

Sit quietly in the meditation of your choosing. Hold your crystal or place it nearby.

MERCURY
RETROGRADE

Mercury Retrograde deserves attention as it's a chance to review your plans and goals. It's notoriously known for causing technology and communication issues, but the upside of this time period is that it offers an invitation to slow down and re-assess where you are and where you want to go.

Fast-moving Mercury symbolizes connection, communication and technology. Mercury is the part of you that learns, thinks, teaches and talks.

Mercury orbits the Sun about four times as fast as the Earth and every time that Mercury zips past the Earth an optical illusion occurs that makes it look as though Mercury is moving backwards. When Mercury appears to be moving backwards (Mercury Retrograde), it's a great opportunity to slow down. Go back over your thoughts and decisions of recent months and review them. Turn inwards to gain guidance from your intuition.

Mercury Retrograde happens about three times a year and lasts for about three weeks each time. You can use these retrograde periods as a moment to check in with yourself and review your practices, thoughts and relationships. Have you been putting off an uncomfortable conversation? Is there something that you need to be honest about with yourself when it comes to relationships, work or money? What has your body been trying to tell you? Is there some new way that you could step out of your comfort zone? What would help you feel more secure and supported?

Underlying issues tend to rise to the surface during Mercury Retrograde. It's typically advised to make sure that you are extra clear in your communications during these periods, and that you wait until the retrograde period has ended before beginning new projects or signing contracts. But it's an excellent time to pick up where you left off on something – to rethink, redo and review.

YOUR CRYSTAL PRACTICE DURING MERCURY RETROGRADE

Crystal energy can help you slow down your busy mind and tune into your intuition during Mercury Retrograde. As you rethink and review, these crystals will amplify your intuition and clarity.

KEEN INSIGHT

Pietersite Employ this speckled Quartz for illuminated insight paired with steady determination.

CLARITY AND COMMUNICATION

Aquamarine This stone soothes and calms the mind while simultaneously boosting your ability to communicate clearly.

CREATIVE THOUGHT

Citrine A crystal that spurs your imagination, helping you conceptualize how you might like patterns or situations to change.

Beginning of Mercury Retrograde Ritual

Perform a full and gentle review of the issues most affecting you by writing a journal entry using the following prompt: 'What do I need to see that I'm not seeing when it comes to my …' Give yourself lots of gratitude in the process and call on your chosen crystal to provide understanding and clarity. When you've finished, write down three takeaways on a small piece of paper and place your crystal on top of it for the remainder of the Retrograde. Drawing on the power of your crystal, let your subconscious mind continue to explore and reveal the subtleties of these thoughts and questions over the coming weeks.

End of Mercury Retrograde Ritual

Near the end of the Retrograde cycle, set an intention to integrate what you've learned during the past days and weeks. Begin by returning to your piece of paper and your crystal. What came up for you during Mercury Retrograde? Was there a new realization, attitude or interest that emerged? Think about what you may have realized and journal about what you'd like to bring into your life now. Is there an intention (see page 22) or affirmation that could come from this exploration? If so, write it down. Look in a mirror and repeat your intention or affirmation five times while holding your crystal. Remember to thank your crystal and to thank yourself for showing up. For the next two weeks, repeat this daily ritual.

CONCLUSION

This book has taken you deep below the Earth's surface, through the metaphorical caverns of crystals and their symbolism. You've connected the dots of the solar system and the meaning of the astrology you were born with. By pairing the forces of the stars above with the crystals below, you've gained tools that can help you navigate your unique journey with wisdom.

In Part Two, you learned about the crystals that can support your unique astrology. This section included insights for Capricorn Sun, Moon and Rising signs, along with supportive crystal recommendations for what your sign needs in five key life areas.

Life is always changing and so in Part Three you learned to follow the energy of the Sun as it moves on its annual journey through the zodiac, finding crystals that may help

you elaborate on the theme of each astrological season.

Revolving and evolving with changing astrological cycles continued in Part Four, where you paired crystal energy with the ebb and flow of the Moon, and learned to harness the power of crystals in tandem with Mercury Retrograde to perform a trimonthly check-in.

All the answers are already within you. When you choose a crystal, you awaken the vibration of that crystal within yourself. Harness your astro-crystal practice to help you see what already exists inside of you. You have everything you need.

With the cosmos above and the crystals below, you are always connected and supported. Let the stones and the stars strengthen your self-awareness and self-trust as you continue your crystalline cosmic journey.

RESOURCES

GET YOUR BIRTH CHART	www.sandysitron.com/crystals
ASTROLOGY READING	www.sandysitron.com
CRYSTALS	***101 Power Crystals:** The Ultimate Guide to Magical Crystals, Gems, and Stones for Healing and Transformation* Judy Hall
CRYSTAL ENERGY HEALING	https://www.kalisaaugustine.com/
SOURCING CRYSTALS RESPONSIBLY	moonrisecrystals.com/
SPIRAL CRYSTALS	spiralcrystals.com/
HOOF AND PAW	hoofandpawuk.com/
ASTROLOGY	***Astrology for Yourself*** Demetra George and Douglas Bloch
AFFIRMATION WORK	Transformational coach Dana Balicki; https://danabalicki.com/
AFFIRMATION WORK	***Empowerment:** The Art of Creating Your Life as You Want It* Gail Straub and David Gershon
ASTROLOGY EDUCATION	www.thestrology.com
	Ritual Enchantments *A Modern Witch's Guide to Self-Possession* Mya Spalter

FEATURED CRYSTALS

LAURENCE KING

First published in Great Britain in 2022 by Laurence King
an imprint of The Orion Publishing Group Ltd
Carmelite House, 50 Victoria Embankment
London EC4Y 0DZ

An Hachette UK Company

10 9 8 7 6 5 4 3 2 1

A CIP catalogue record for this book is
available from the British Library.

ISBN 978-0-8578-2925-2

Design: Therese Vandling

Printed in China by C&C Offset Printing Co. Ltd

Laurence King Publishing is committed to ethical and
sustainable production. We are proud participants in the
Book Chain Project®. [bookchainproject.com]

www.laurenceking.com
www.orionbooks.co.uk